A Softer Kind of Audacity
Jess Whetsel

Praise for

A Softer Kind of Audacity

"Love is a softer kind of audacity / like this bouquet of pink-petaled / fireworks in my hands." writes Jess Whetsel in this moving debut. Here, love in all its forms — platonic, polyamorous, ancestral, and self — are woven into a welcome mat that invites the reader back into their bodies. Whetsel understands that one must "be patient; it may take you some time to arrive" and so invites us into the journey of return, where "even my detours dazzle me." *A Softer Kind of Audacity* reminds us that reclaiming our power and joy are not only possible, but necessary.

- Amanda Roth, author of
A Mother's Hunger

A Softer Kind of Audacity is the perfect title for this tender yet powerful collection of poems. Jess writes with the honesty and bravery of a human longing to fully recognize her self. A self that took time and tears and breathtaking vulnerability to unearth. She does not leave a single stone unturned on her path to wholeness, freedom, and reclamation, and her work invites you deeply in. This is an extraordinary collection of poetry.

- Kate Mapother, author of
Tell Me You Hear the Riot

Whetsel captures so much imagery and makes simple objects we rarely pay attention to important. I can never look at a door frame the same. She is a painter who was never given a brush. Thankfully she stumbled upon a pen.

- Irina Bogomolova, author of
They Will Not Bleed for Us

Whetsel's poetry is like a hand, gently guiding her readers through the rolling landscapes of coming home to oneself. She has a way of naming that which hasn't yet been named - or rather, naming the things we haven't yet dared to name for ourselves, but that have always lingered just below the surface. *A Softer Kind of Audacity* feels at once like an invitation, an invocation, and a soft place to land. I look forward to returning to these words often.

- Jenn Stark, writer

A Softer Kind of Audacity offers soothing whispers as much as it does brilliant shouts. Raw and personal, the poetry reaches out to be touched, the aches shared with and the joy gifted to the reader. Whetsel holds nothing back, writing a study of self under a lens that offers itself up to the reader as a mirror, and creating a love story out of many parts.

- Kathryn Moon, author of
A Lady of Rooksgrave Manor
and *Sanctuary with Kings*

I love the balance of humor, playfulness, and wit, as well as the darker and more serious topics. The way Whetsel tackles taboo subjects is graceful, informative, and inspiring... I can't wait until the world gets to read *A Softer Kind of Audacity.*

- Kennedi Jones, author of
incandescent

Whetsel explores themes like queerness and body dysmorphia with a relatability that reels you in and a specificity that stings. This collection is cohesive and each word choice feels deliberate as well as relevant to the overall message. All in all, this is a winner.

- April Renee, poet

A Softer Kind of Audacity

Cover art: Bobbi Stark www.bobbistark.com
Editor: Frances Story (Poet Jen Harris) www.writingworkshopkc.com
Formatting: Samantha Peters

ISBN: 979-8-9889819-0-9

This book is for the little girl with
wild curls and a poem in her heart;
the teenager who scribbled lyrics in her
notebook like her life depended on it;
the twenty-something who swallowed her voice
and didn't think she'd ever write again;
and the woman who finally came home
to her poetry, her voice, her self.

We did it, baby.
We did it.

Table of Contents

How to Come Home to Yourself, No Matter How Far You've Strayed

Light a candle; build the fire; burn some incense.

Sweep your front porch; shake out your welcome mat.

Fill the kettle with water and place it on the stovetop to boil – or simply microwave a mug; you have come too far to be particular.

Prepare the tea leaves, a few kinds; you cannot predict what will soothe your soul until you see yourself in the doorframe.

What else would you offer an honored guest? A bowl of fruit; a bouquet of dandelions from your overgrown yard; your own arms, open and yearning? Make the necessary preparations. Follow your heart.

Sit by your fire and wait. Be patient; it may take you some time to arrive.

When you hear the shuffling steps, the nervous knock, rise and open the door.

Smile, no matter how weary or ragged or gaunt you may appear, even if you do not recognize yourself.

Say *hello*.

Say *I have been waiting for this day to come.*

Say *I am sorry*, if you need to.

Say *I love you*.

Say *come in, come in, please make yourself at home.*

Hang up your coat, take off your shoes.

Offer your comfiest seat.

Sit close and hold hands.

Say *I love you* again.

Say *thank you for coming home.*

The Patron Saint of Writing

She is curiosity come alive,
with tangled curls and a heart
like James's giant peach –
big enough to house her whole world,
vulnerable to bruising,
and a little bit magic.

Her mouth moves noiselessly
as she scribbles across the page;
she is unaware that she does this
when the universe speaks through her.

She has just written her first poem,
a little ditty about a tree,
her favorite pine in the yard
whose branches form the staircase
to her secret hideaway, the place
she feels safe to be herself.

Until today, she was just a child.
But now, she knows her power.

Hanging Out with a Younger Version of Myself

When I feel you in my heart
I cue up a playlist
carefully curated
for moments like these.

The tracks shuffle
and so do the years.
Here we are in middle school
when our crush asked us to dance
and our heart stopped for
four minutes and thirty-six seconds.
Here we are as a child
with wild curls and a watermelon dress
and *mmmbop!* blaring on the boombox.
Here we are in daddy's pickup truck
kicking our little legs in the sunshine
singing along to Tom Petty.
Here we are in the wake of our first breakup
crying in the middle of the night
with headphones on.

Here we are in our first car
driving too fast in the dark
blasting Jimmy Eat World.
Here we are in our spiral staircase tree
with books and Beanie Babies.
Here we are in our twenties
with a roadmap that's just a question mark
and a gaping hole in our chest.
Here, we are.

This is my favorite kind of time travel,
riding sound waves into past lives,
and as the music swells I feel you
reaching out into the future,
eyes full of unknowns,
and as I sing along
I promise you:
we're still here, sweet one,
and everything is okay.

Grown-Up Shit

I am at once too old
and too young for
all this grown-up shit.
The heaviness of the world
crushes me and I reach out
for Disney movies, Backstreet Boys,
bean dip and queso. I reach
back through time and space
but never fully recapture the ease,
just a fleeting nostalgic stupor,
a momentary dissociation.
I reach for youth in the same breath
as I denigrate it, thank everything holy
that I no longer occupy that body,
or the hellscape of the early aughts –
just this fresh one that keeps me reaching.

I go out to eat with my husband
on a Saturday night and as we
pay the check, the waitress asks
about our plans for the evening.

I say, "going home and putting on
stretchy pants," and she laughs in
that uneasy way twenty-somethings do
when they catch a glimpse of
their future selves in the wild.

The night is young and I am not.
I go home and put on those pants
and crawl into bed with a hip that
keeps tapping me on the shoulder.
I am too young for this problem
and I am too old for all the others,
the horrors of living this life
in this reality, in these inconceivable
ways we've shaped it to be.

Ode to My Curls

i.

My father's gift to me
was a head full
of dark, lustrous curls.
He likes to joke
that his own fell out
after I was born,
a torch he never meant to pass.

Tendrils twirled into cascading corkscrews
that framed my face and
mystified my mother
whose deliberate brush strokes
taught me that beauty is pain.

I moved through the world
as a circus sideshow,
a cesspool of unsolicited opinions.
Everyone always had something to say:
accuse them of being fake,
tell me I should feel lucky,

advise me to straighten them,
tease my frizzy coils, or worse,
wrap one around their finger without asking
lest I forget that
I am woman
I am exotic
I am public.

I couldn't help but wonder
what life would be like without them
announcing my presence to a world
I wished would grant me peace.

ii.

The electric razor hums;
the mirror makes me a stranger.
I only see my grandmother there,
her pixie cut speckled eggshell-white,
her high cheekbones,
her full pink lips.

My grandmother,
who never said "I love you"
even when she still had words.

My grandmother,
a mere flicker of light left
behind her cloudy eyes.
My grandmother,
the mystery.

I grow weary
of not recognizing
my own reflection.
I worry
that I too
could elude my loved ones,
that I too
could be unknowable.
I cannot think
of a worse way to live.

iii.

My soul yearns to be known,
even when it doesn't.
And so I speak my truths aloud
when I discover them
in the clearing of my heart.

I uncover myself
beneath layers of caked dust
and old, rotten stories.
I work hard to know myself,
and it helps a little,
on those days I blink once, twice
before recognizing my own eyes.

It helps a little
to remember that
I am not a mystery
even when I feel like one
as my body shape-shifts through time,

laugh lines kissing the corners of my eyes
and grays sprouting from my scalp.
My curls have been there through it all
whether I liked it or not:
my safety blanket
twined 'round my fingers,
my conjoined twin,
my evergreen.

Today they are just long enough
to loop at my earlobes,
little half-moon hairs
that dance in the breeze.
I ache for them
to grow long again
and fall into my face
just to remind me they're alive,
blossoming, voluminous, and free –
and so am I.

Compost

after "From the House of Yemanjá" by Audre Lorde

I have two faces and a flower pot
filled with stale soil and wood chips
and a sprinkle of coffee grounds.

I have two faces and one cradles
my failures in her hands, watches
them writhe like worms before
spiraling into the dirt. She pulls
a seed from her pocket, presses it
into the earth with her thumb,
rubs her palms to dispel the dust.

I have two faces and the other
turns away to hide her shame.
She only wants the bright bloom,
does not see the magic in burying
her grief, misses the tiny green tendril
already sprouting from the kernel
of her cracked-open dreams.

I have two faces and one says
it's just a flower pot; the other
calls it her lineage of hope.

Afterlife

I did not learn your name
until I was a teenager. It was
an accident, a slip of another
relative's tongue, something
I wasn't supposed to hear –
or at least not from their lips:
my secret grandfather,
the villain of the family story.

The rest came later, in pieces.
You left because you fell in love
with a man after three children
with your wife. You left because
you could no longer pretend
you were the man you claimed to be.
But I am the author of the family
and I am rewriting this story.
You left because you had
the audacity to choose yourself.

I doubt my father meant to
keep his queer daughter
from her only living queer kin,
but that is what he did. And now
you are dead, your ashes interred
in a scenic cemetery states away
from this hole in my heart and
the corn fields and country roads
you left behind. But that is not all you left.

When I miss you the most, I look
in the mirror. Here is your Mona Lisa
smile on my mouth, your blunt-tipped
nose on my face. I place my hand on
my heart and feel the swagger of your
footsteps. I reach out, skin on silver,
to stroke the arch of your cheekbone.
No one can take you from me.
You are still here because I am
still breathing, and I promise
you will not be erased.

happy fatality

your blue eyes turned to steel
as I looked up from your note
full of questions that
had nothing to do with
your disaster handwriting
(the sacred script
in which I was fluent)

you were my first mirror
a live wire, a heart on fire
every cell of you hummed
with electric emotion
and I knew how it felt
to drown in your own well
to be "much too" everything

our friendship became
our safe place to land
to confess everything
except the one thing
neither of us had words for

I slept in your bed
with your hand in mine
you told me you loved me
until my mother
raised her eyebrows
and it would be years
before I understood
that you meant it
and so did I
and you were afraid
of what that meant
we deserved better
than secret kisses
in a middle school bathroom

we deserved more
space to explore
time to bask
in that purest of love
to shine on each other
and illuminate our truth

instead we worked
with what little we had
crushed on a pair of brothers
and dreamed of a life
as sisters (in law)
always together
in a way
my heart knew
was second-best

I still don't understand
how everything changed
why you wrote the words
that trembled in my hands
as you kissed me goodbye

do best friends kiss? you asked
we do, I said
maybe they shouldn't, you whispered

then you left me alone
on the bathroom tiles
and I think part of me
is there even now
lips still buzzing
with your electricity

Platonic Love

There is a room in my heart
that only you can enter. You forged
a key from curiosity and devotion, tied it
'round your neck with fishing line, but still
you knock first, let me open the door.
I welcome you in with a checkerboard grin.

Once inside, time rewinds,
smooths the lines on your face.
Adulthood is a heavy wool coat
you leave crumpled on the floor.
You take my tiny hand in yours
and it feels like watching a rainstorm
from a covered porch, like the
soft pink belly of an animal.

How tender this love,
unlike any other.
How limited our lexicon
for the spectrum of intimacy.

How beautiful the truth
that is never too late –
that play is your birthright,
that it longs for a mate.

Stitchmates

She rarely moves,
stitching in stillness,
living the life she has
made for herself
inside my home.

I would never say it aloud
but I am terrified of her,
no matter how small
or insignificant she may seem
in the grand scheme of things.

We do not speak,
except for the days I feel brave
and quip as I breeze past her,
"The rent was due on the first,
so, y'know, anytime would be great."

This is how we joke,
as if she'd applied months ago
with her spider credit score,
as if she'd ever asked my permission
to nest in the corner beside my plants.

Change asks for forgiveness, not permission.
No call ahead, no knock on the door,
just a stubborn, sudden arrival
and the ensuing shock of realizing
you were not promised a damn thing.

So I do my best to keep going
as though my home was ever truly safe.
I take up crochet for the hell of it
and together we weave in the sunlight,
ten eyes, twelve legs, two hearts.

Oh, hio

i.

Before daybreak stretches over
floorboards, crawls into our bed,
luxuriates on my naked pillow;
before you wake in the empty dawn,
I am gone.

I drive through fields, rolling hills
of corn and sunflowers and wheat,
tall grasses rippling in the wind.
The cerulean sky sinks down to earth,
settles upon the river of tar, sprawls
before me like an upside-down ocean.
I cup my hands and drink the air,
syrupy-thick, honey dripping
from the clouds, pine notes
wafting down the tree-freckled
mountains that rise up ahead.
I let your name become a memory.

ii.

I return to you,
an unfaithful lover
creeping back into
your darkened house.
Your name is a sigh
as it escapes my lips,
a reluctant whisper.

Against my will, I am called
back to your familiar embrace.
You know me, know how often
I have strayed, though you do not
keep count. We lay together,
consumed by night, moonlight
lapping at the foot of our bed.
I close my eyes and all I see
are sea-blue skies, shadows
of cumulus clouds speckling
green mountain sides.

The Ocean Has Taken Me as a Lover

The ocean has taken me
as a lover, which is to say
I let her crash into me
over and over again

At her shoreline in the sunshine
she licks the tips of my toes
begs me to come in deeper
to drown in her desire

I wade in slowly, taking my time
though she froths and foams
demanding my submission
to her rise-and-fall horizon

She churns and swells beneath me
My fingers skim the surface
of her undulating curves
I succumb to her currents

And when she's had her way with me
she spits me out in a riptide
leaves me gasping for air
sticky with sweat and sand

She swallows the sun to bring on the night
beckons the moon and we bask in its light
With saltwater kisses, she sings me to sleep
We both know that I am not hers to keep

I stumble back to my life on wobbly legs
the waters of my body still aswirl
and I find myself landlocked
with a drought in my heart

The World Is All Gates

and I am walking through the airport,
trying to decide which plane to board.
Voices ping-pong along the concourse,
announcements for imminent departures.
I can board any plane I choose,
but that's just it –
I have to choose.

I rush past a gate for publication.
First class is boarding a plane
headed to motherhood; the woman
scanning tickets gestures at me urgently.
There is a gate for another degree,
one for taking over the flower farm,
one for the lesbian love affair of my dreams.

Some destinations have multiple flights a day;
others are one-time opportunities.
I never know until I board.

The moving walkway tugs
at my feet, an undertow pulling me
to a windowed lounge with chairs and outlets
and a sign that reads *Stay the Course.*
When I am overwhelmed by my options,
which is often, I sit in a plush chair
with an egg McMuffin and wait.

Alternate Lives

i.

I am a sea witch on the California coast. I take many lovers, but
live alone. My little white-fenced yard is bursting with life: stray
cats and succulents and sky lupine. The flower garden has
survived every season of wildfire – a miracle, or perhaps just a spell.

ii.

I trust the nervous whispers of my heart, the lick of fire in my
belly. We marry young, make a home for ourselves in the country.
I build a trellis, train a rose bush to climb it, bring her cuttings of
creamy orange blooms just like her daddy used to do.

iii.

I am loyal to a fault. While my first love snores, I lay awake and
think of all the exits I've passed on this highway to hell, turning
up the radio to drown out the sound of my soul crying for
escape. Now there are no more off-ramps, just one lane of asphalt
stretching through the desert. The roadside wildflowers reach for
me, but it is too late.

iv.

I almost board the plane, but at the last second, I turn around. I rent a room on my favorite cobblestoned street, the one the wisteria took over, lavender sequins dripping from winding vines. The ghost of my American accent only haunts me when my mother is on the phone.

Winter

Darkness swallows the trees
behind my house by suppertime.
The cold has silenced our once-chatty creek;
the birds have flown the coop.
Barren, scraggly branches stretch
towards perpetual twilight while horse
chestnuts rot in the undergrowth.

I find myself feeling like a child again –
alone with my thoughts in an unlit room.
My mind races with visions
I struggle to pin down with my pen.
I vacuum my floors with the ghost
of a gun pressed to my temple.
There is nothing to do but wait.

Triggered

My stomach churns,
trying to climb my ribcage
like a ladder, but my chest
is so tight and taut
that it just gets stuck there,
wedged between my lungs.

My thoughts are a tornado,
spiraling through space,
too fast to be understood.

My heart sits in silence.
It cannot be swayed
by my anxious mind,
now turning my cavernous skull
into a puppet theater,
passionately acting out the lines
it stole from childhood bullies
and former lovers
and rehearsed until
it knew them by heart.

My heart beats faster
but does not say a word.
It does not have to.
I know its pulsing ache;
I felt the moment it backed up
against my spine and sank,
an overwhelmed child
sliding down to the floor.

My heart waits patiently
until my mind exhausts itself,
runs out of excuses,
speaks all its words,
finishes the montage of memories.
And then, in spacious silence,
my heart speaks slowly
until my whole body
reverberates with truth.

Assessment of Grief

NAME: Jess	very likely	some what likely	some what unlikely	very unlikely
Lately I'm grateful my heart is caged by my ribs	X			
It wails like a coyote at the full round moon		X		
Press an ear to my chest, you will hear its lament			X	
It is hard to be a human with a soul so feral	X			
I did not ask to be alive in this dying world	X			
But I keep waking up here so I guess this is it			X	
I long for the endless expanse of the unknown		X		
Laying on the closet floor will do for now			X	
Yes, I am hiding; no, I do not want to be found				X
The tender timbre of your voice cracks me open	X			
And I am scared of what will spill out of me		X		
My heart is too wild to be set free				X

Trauma

I have decided
to call you
by your name.

To speak the word
I never used because
my scars are invisible.

To believe myself
when I say
I was abused.

I have decided
to call you
by your name

and now something
has changed. I meet
your gaze when

I look back, unwavering.
You do not scare me; I know
the only way out is through.

I have decided
to call you
by your name

and sometimes
I wish I hadn't become
another poet turned

trauma pornographer,
recreating the gruesome scene,
immortalizing your cruelty.

I have decided
to call you
by your name

and get on with
my life, because
I know now

I am real love,
the kind that heals
the deepest wounds.

Nude Beach

I come home from the nude beach
and tell my husband about the man
old enough to be my father
who bet I'd make a good wife
with a body like that
who laid back in the sand
dick tucked between his thighs
and watched me put my clothes back on
piece by piece
made my stomach turn and my chest tighten
until I was safe in my car
until the click of the lock
until I finally exhaled

I tell my husband about the man
old enough to be my father
like sharing what I had for breakfast
I watch him brace for tears
that never seem to come
no matter how many men
old enough to be my father
there are

(And that's just the ones
who are old enough to be my father)
A lifetime of being catcalled
touched without my consent
undressed by a leering gaze
becomes a grocery list of assaults
I can recite without blinking

I am worried
by how numb I have become
that I do not call myself a victim
because I know so many people
who lost so much more
than their comfort

How long will I draw
these lines in the sand?

Dysmorphia

I wish there was some way
to make her see me.

When she does look at me,
her brow furrows; she squints;
her lips pucker to the side.
She pinches my folds
and I remember the way
she used to grip them
with scissored fingers
and dream of cutting me
like a paper snowflake.
She turns to the side
and examines my belly,
sucks in to flatten,
softens it round again
with a heavy sigh.

Why can't she see my legs,
strong enough to march her
toward her wildest dreams?

Why must she make a secret
of my starlight smile?
Why does she ignore my heart,
the ticking clock that grants her
breath and life and love?

I have become a list of slurs
her tongue borrowed from other mouths.
She hides me in baggy sweatshirts
when all I want is to be seen.
She feeds me scraps, withholds
flavors that bring me joy, obsesses
over every morsel, has nightmares
about where each bite will live in me.

And all the while, I am working,
conducting this orchestra of organs,
wishing she could hear the symphonies
they sing in her honor.
All the while, I am wondering
if it will ever be good enough for her –
the chemical reactions I conjure,
the magic I weave to get her out of bed
each bright, new morning.
I give and give and give
but all she sees of me are
the pieces she'd like to destroy.

A Dreamless Sleep

I knew about halfway through –
it was less of a relationship
and more of a mothering.
I picked up your discarded socks
before friends came over, turned off
the stove when you forgot. I paid
for every meal and month of rent
so you could live your dream,
tucking mine beneath my pillow
for a drowsy stretch of time.

If you'd asked me if I was happy,
I would have tipped my head like
you'd slipped into another language.
But I loved you, or at least I was
pretty sure I did, and if anything better
was even out there at all, it wasn't
meant for me. I loved you, and
I hated the mechanics of us.
I didn't yet know a woman
with a different story.

I swallowed my resentments
like a collection of knives
lest I turn them on you or
press their edges to my skin.
I kept my hibernating rage
asleep. I did these things
until they stopped working.
I woke, belly full of blades,
and remembered: I am alive,
and that is not a mistake.

Thank You

for leaving your mark on my work
without my consent

for teaching me
the importance of boundaries

I still hang that painting on my wall
just so I can remember

the tug-of-war tension
between collaboration

and domination

This Body

round, rolling mounds
of sand dune skin
ancient redwood limbs
a barren landscape
where hair once bloomed
new aches, strange creaks
streams of stretch marks
and rivulets of wrinkles

when this body feels foreign
I press my palms to its flesh
and call it *home*

The Lunar Light Within

I am learning
to see myself
as the moon

To honor my phases
of light and shadow
To dance to the cadence
of the song within me
To surrender to the cycle
of blood and creation
spontaneous combustion
rebirth within the flames

I am learning
to see myself
as the moon

Always whole
even when I only
show the part of myself
that is luminous

The part of me that believes
I will get through this
The part of me that trusts
in the silent rhythms
that guided generations
of ancestors before me

I am learning
to see myself
as the moon

Perfect because of
my imperfections
not despite them
The bumps and craters
on the surface
the topographical map
of my life
Each rise and fall
a daily reminder
that I am still breathing

I am learning
to see myself
as the moon

Even when the night sky
envelops me in black velvet
and I am caught in the currents
of my spiraling mind
I tread water until the sunlight
stretches over the horizon
and a sliver of me shines through
to light my way back home

The Stars Talk About Us, Too

and wonder aloud
why a lifeform with such potential
would squander their evanescent existence
in the dusty bed of a pickup truck
staring up at the velveteen sky.

Multiple Choice for the Grieving Heart

after "Multiple Choice for Adrift Michigander" by Brian Czyzyk

How can one survive a season of grief?

A. Surrender completely; allow yourself to be consumed. Eaten alive. Let it take bite after bite until you are nothing but bone and rotting scraps of flesh. Wait for the vultures. Wait for the wind. Wait for whatever comes next.

B. Fill the vessel of your body with literally anything else: black curlicues of smoke, blood-red wine, midnight Taco Bell. Tell your bloated grief that your guest house is full. Let it pace outside your front door.

C. Collect the empty bottles from the recycling bin, your grandmother's china that never gets used, a baseball bat. Take your brittle bounty to an empty field. Unhinge your vocal cords and scream at the darkening sky. Peer into the mirror of broken glass and fall for the feral glow in your bloodshot eyes.

D. Imagine that your grief is a shrieking infant. Cradle it in your aching arms; croon a tune someone once sang to you. Resist the urge to shake it into submission; put it down and walk away for a moment, if you must. Return to its side when you are ready. Try to love it even while it is wailing. Whisper that you have no idea what you're doing, but you're doing your best.

Where Did I Get My Heart From?

after "Still Here" by Kyron Rashād

My heart is a hand-me-down
from my ancestors brave enough
to pave a new path for their progeny.
My heart is a hummingbird, a hailstorm,
a hyacinth. My heart is a vining plant,
climbing up, rooting down, push-and-pull,
tug-of-war. My heart is an open door,
a red carpet reaching for your cold feet.
My heart is a radio tower broadcasting live
my full emotional spectrum for your entertainment
among intermittent ads for cat food and
weight loss supplements. My heart is
a portal to an alternate universe where
we speak a common language
that has no word for *fear.*

Leap of Faith

When stopped, staring blankly
at a crossroads
I stroll down the path
that reminds me least
of myself, winding away
from all I have worked for.

When stopped, staring blankly
into the mirror
I avoid my eyes
like sunken caves,
the color drained from my skin,
a flatline personified.

The body always knows
what the heart and mind
are often last to discover:
the winds are changing course
and it's time to hoist your sails,
though you are weary
and the journey is treacherous.

Today I stood at the edge
of my own cliff
and was surprised to see
myself at the bottom,
a foggy reflection
of a me I don't yet know.
Her eyes burned through the mist
like she held a truth inside her
that could set my world ablaze.

I took a deep breath
and dove head-first
into myself.

I want to know
what she knows.

What It Is That I Am

I am a woman who loves
a man and a woman. I am
liminal space, the in-between,
the not-this and not-that.
I am indefinable, although we
made up a name for what it is
that I am. I did not speak it
until I'd lived for thirty years.
I had not lived at all –
not until that moment.
I birthed myself with tongue
and teeth, four syllables
my sanctuary.

I have known it all my life, but
knowing is different than living –
a prerequisite, perhaps, but not
the same animal. I have always
been this creature, and yet
I am not the same animal.

I slept for decades, dreamed
a world, believed it was real.
Then I awoke to the sound
of a word I never let myself fit
inside of but always felt like
home, familiar and safe.

This Season of Life

Find me caressing the leaves of every plant I see,
learning their names, telling them mine.
Find me buttoned up in flannel by day,
draped in velvet and lace by night.
Find me in the kitchen stirring a pot
clockwise with a wooden spoon.
Find me barefoot in the backyard,
eyes closed, face turned to the sun.
Find me remembering to water my garden
but forgetting to feed myself. Find me
filling notebooks, spilling tea, ankle-deep
in the creek. Find me catching spiders
in a cup instead of crushing them
with my foot. Find me collecting cat
whiskers in a shot glass on my altar.
Find me with a joint between my lips,
wrapped in a halo of wispy smoke.
Find me on my back porch listening
to the rain. Find me wailing with my
knees clutched to my chest. Find me
laughing with my head tipped back
so the sky can see my joy.

The Essentials
Jess Whetsel: writer, killjoy,
hacker of menstrual cycles

after Tom Ford & Seneca Basoalto

1. Three browser windows, each holding at least eight open tabs

2. Vases of cut flowers in every room of the house

3. An iced decaf lavender oat milk latte
   I don't care if it reduces me to a meme

4. A misplaced mothering instinct showered upon
   cats and houseplants

5. Shelves straining to hold all the books I've bought
   and have yet to read

6. A sheet pan spread with individually-prepared nachos
   Each chip is a perfect specimen; this, to me, is love

7. A journal for journaling, a journal for poems,
   a journal for cycle tracking

8. Ginger ale poured from the can into a glass with no ice

9. Twirling my hair when I don't
   know what else to do with my hands
   It's not cute, it's a coping mechanism

10. A bold swipe of hot magenta lipstick

11. Synthetic diamonds and Mexican fire opals

12. A glittery mint green pickup truck named Rita
    Give your inner child what she wants, girl

13. Every card I've ever received in a box in my closet

14. Dopamine hits in order of preference:
    sunlight, cheese, Target run

15. Talking to the trees along the park path
    They're the best listeners I know

"What is enlightenment, anyway?"

It's the way my soul recognized you
immediately, sensed you were kindred,
dragged me by the hand across the room
so I could learn your name. How I was drawn
to your light, a lost ship in the dark catching
its first glimpse of home. The way I knew
before I had any way of knowing. How quickly
admiration blossomed into adoration and
curdled my stomach into champagne quicksand.
It's how you see me so clearly that we go backward
in time until my child self is standing before you,
and how lovingly you crouch before her
and hold her hand. It's the press of your cheek
against mine, the way our bodies notch together
like they know they are a pair. It's letting you
crack open my simple life like a wrecking ball,
and finding the missing pieces of my heart
among the rubble. It's trusting that taking
your hand won't set my bridges ablaze.

It's my still and spacious chest,
even as my life morphs into something
unfamiliar and dazzlingly beautiful.
It's the way I stumbled upon your heart
like a door in my house I've never seen before,
the way loving you feels like opening it
and stepping into a whole new world,
but I'm still home.

Double Life

It started with the pink Power Ranger.
I loathed the color of her unitard,
despised her boring blonde hair,
but I couldn't stop watching her
and I didn't know why.

It started with my 8th grade best friend.
We wrote letters swearing
we'd always be together.
We held hands and said "I love you"
before hanging up the phone
and shared scaredy-cat smooches.
One day she declared our friendship was over
and I didn't know why.

It started with Carmen Elektra.
I hated her, and it was only sort of because
my boyfriend jerked off to her photos.
Her body filled me with rage
and I didn't know why.

It started with the first porno I ever watched.
My eyes never left the actress's breasts.
I admitted this to a friend on a laugh laced with shame,
but she told me that was normal; women can look
at other women without being, well, *you know.*
A quiet anger stirred in the cavern of my belly
and I didn't know why.

It started with the redheaded captain of my college crew team.
A teammate and I giggled that we had a "girl crush" on her,
but we weren't, like, *attracted* to her or anything,
we just adored everything she did and said and wore,
we just wanted to be her friend, we just wanted to *be* her
and we didn't know why.

It started with coming out to my husband,
who joined me in mourning the versions of me
who never got to be who they really were –
the present one included.
My husband, who I swore to love forever,
a promise I do not want to break.

My husband, who told me tearfully
that he only stands to benefit from me being whole,
that he will not let his own fear be my next oppressor.
It started with an invisible string
tugging me across the room
until I found myself at her side,
high on her floral saffron perfume,
asking if we could be friends.
Weeks later, she put her hand on my leg
while we laughed together,
and some small, shadowy creature within me
woke up after years of silent sleep,
and finally, *finally,* I knew.

POLYAMORY IS THE ULTIMATE FORM OF HEALING AND NO I WILL NOT ELABORATE

I am not the same since I discovered
that I am too beautiful, too magical,
too desirable a treasure to be hoarded.
That a wealth such as myself must be shared.
That I can trust in the infinite abundance of love,
that its purest expression is freedom.

I am not the same since I received
all the touch my younger self yearned for.
"Too much" and "not enough" no longer circle
my heart like vultures. I don't eat myself sick
when what needs nourishment is my soul.
I smile at my soft belly, my small breasts.

I am not the same since I remembered
that my love is not a pie to be quantified or quartered
but a bonfire, an ever-expanding blaze
illuminating the endless night of existence.

Making Love

Back in college, I wrote in my diary,
"Sometimes I feel like sex is something greater
than I know what to do with, something sanctified
that I am demeaning, something I shouldn't be doing
because I don't really know what it *means*
when two bodies come together."

I had no way of knowing that I was having
the worst sex of my life, sex with a man
who asked me not to look into his eyes like that,
who worried too much about the bulge of my belly,
who thought about other women when he was inside me.
I was having sex with him because I loved him,
for some reason, and because he claimed to love me.

Back then I used to cringe at the phrase "making love."
That was so long ago, back when I thought I knew
what love was. Before the first time you smiled at me
and I heard the ancient soul within me whisper, "Pay attention."
Before I learned how it feels to be seen, to see another,
to see them seeing you. Before I knew orgasm as the universe
swallowing me whole while your full moon eyes blaze in the dark.

Later in life, I read that sex is how adults play together
and the child within me didn't feel so lonely anymore.
Still, some days I find myself saying to you, longingly,
that I wish we could have known each other
when we were young.
You smile back at me, a wistful look on your face.
Then we make love.

Question of the Day

What's something I don't know about you?

All my life I yearned for the kind of bosom friend
that Anne of Green Gables had found in Diana –
an open heart, a hand to hold, a *kindred spirit.*
But female fellowship felt more like a minefield,
never knowing which step would be my last.
I stanched my bleeding heart through the explosions
until finally I raised the white flag, let men become
my harbor, pruned the girly suffix from my name.

*If you could see any mythical creature in the wild
and know it was real, what would you want to see?*

I am beholding you now: my long-lost sister-soulmate.
Ever since I was a child, I always believed in you.
Even on the nights when doubt kept me from sleep,
I clung to my hope like a security blanket that someday
I would stumble upon your saffron scent and mermaid curls.
In the darkness I would pinch my skin,
take comfort in the pain;
as long as I was real, I knew you must be, too.

What food and drink would represent your
body and blood in a communion ceremony?

We learned each other's hearts over
queso and margaritas, gyros and Coke,
pad see ew and sparkling water.
I knew it was love when I realized
all our bodies want to do is share:
clothes, snacks, hair clips, secrets, laughter, stories, desire.
I knew it was love when I realized
life tastes better when you're at the table.

Morning Glory

I want a Sunday morning kind of love.
A linger in our bed a little longer kind of love.
A love like a full-body cat stretch,
toe beans spread wide. Like fresh air
through the open window, the whispered
hum of a ceiling fan. A love that vines
towards the sky, that blooms with the sunrise.

I want the kind of love that has
nowhere to go today. Love like a homemade
latte, like a slice of the pizza
we forgot to put away. A love that meanders
through the house like soft jazz on vinyl. I want
a cuddled up together on the couch kind of love.
A *how did you sleep last night* kind of love,
a *look babe there's a new leaf* kind of love,
a *tell me about the book you're reading* kind of love.

I want a spontaneous shower sex kind of love,
a steal your hoodie kind of love. A love that
plans meals for the week, makes a list,
gets high on the way to the store. I want
a love that wanders the aisles, that sings
along to the crackling radio. The kind of love
that chats up the Girl Scouts, buys boxes
of cookies just because.
I want a kiss at every stoplight kind of love.
A windows down, hold my hand kind of love.
A *let's go home* kind of love.

A Softer Kind of Audacity

I find myself shaking when I read the news these days.
My hands tremble as I take the world in, worst-first.
It feels like spoon-feeding myself toxic sludge.
It sits like a stone in my belly amongst the rising tides
of bile and acid. There is only so much I can stomach
before I have to lie down like a Victorian woman on a fainting sofa,
the back of one hand kissing my damp forehead,
the other arm lolling towards the floor like a corpse limb.

This is the part where I want to cry,
but I am too numb to make tears.
I've been here enough to know
they won't come when it's convenient.
They will lie in wait until suddenly
they are streaming down my face
as my feline soulmate nestles in the crook of my arm,
after perfect sex with the love of my life,
while I clip blushing peonies in spring sunlight.

There is still plenty of good in the world,
but I have to want to see it, like peering
through the haze of a Magic Eye
for a glimpse of clarity. I have to stoop
to hear it over the sound of everything else
fighting for a fraction of my limited attention span.

All I know is that hate is loud
but lacks substance.
Love is a softer kind of audacity,
like this bouquet of pink-petaled
fireworks in my hands.

There is still plenty of good in the world.
I just have to reach for it.

Prayer

May I stand in my full power
May I respect and honor myself
May I care for my beautiful vessel
and follow the heart that beats within it
May I get still enough to listen
for the voice of my highest self
May I trust her above all others

May my gut pave the way forward
May even my detours dazzle me with scenery
May I recognize the breadcrumbs I left behind
when I stumble upon my path again

May I be a creative conduit
still enough to distill the divine into words
May I be vulnerable enough to set them free
so the world can see
me

May I have the courage to speak my truth
and honor it no matter how it is received
May I be fearless enough to become
who I am meant to be

May I allow myself to fail
and let it mean nothing
May I do things that I am not good at
yet bring me immense joy
May freedom electrify my body
spark me up like a string of lights
May I revel in the pleasure
of lifelong learning

May I dance naked in the rain
May I sing songs that haven't been written yet
May I speak to myself with love and patience
May I embrace my wholeness
May I love and be loved

May I let my heart shatter
and glue the pieces back together
again and again and again
May it only make me stronger
more loving, more present

May I remember that each person I meet
is a teacher, a mirror, a gift
May I remember that we are all connected

May I surround myself with those
who love me and want to grow with me
May we thrive and rise together
May our community garden flourish

May I trust that I am here on purpose
May I always come home to my purpose
May I rest enough to dream of miracles
and be awake enough to make them reality

May I put in the work
from a place of love
May I put in the work
even when I don't feel like it

May I divest from all that keeps me
small and stagnant and safe
May I divest from all that keeps us
shackled within these harmful systems
May we all be free

May I know peace
May I know ease
May I give them to myself
May I share them with others
May I share all that I have

May I be more of myself
than I ever thought possible

Crown Yourself

You secret celebration,
you wild song.
You fresh revolution,
you naturally-born dream,
you power source.

Embrace your whole being;
honor every phase. Promise me
you will love yourself
you will plant yourself here
you will be gentle
you will let yourself thrive

and your creativity blossom
and take pleasure in the way
the world stops to admire
the sheer force
of you.

NOTES

"The Patron Saint of Writing," "The world is all gates," "Winter," "Triggered," "A Dreamless Sleep," "What It Is That I Am," "What is enlightenment, anyway?", "Double Life," and "A Softer Kind of Audacity" are based on prompts from Jen Harris' The Writing Workshop KC (@poetjenharris, @writingworkshopkc).

"Compost" is written after "From the House of Yemanjá" by Audre Lorde, published in *The Collected Poems of Audre Lorde*, 1997; and is based on a prompt from Seneca Basoalto (@senecabasoalto).

"happy fatality" was previously published in *Out of the Darkness, Into the Light: Writing Workshop KC Anthology, Volume I*, 2022.

"Platonic Love," "POLYAMORY IS THE ULTIMATE FORM OF HEALING AND NO I WILL NOT ELABORATE," and "Morning Glory" are based on prompts from Seneca Basoalto (@senecabasoalto).

"Alternate Lives" is based on a prompt from Amy Kay (@amykaypoetry).

"Assessment of Grief" is written after "Bunny's Questionnaire" by Bunny Boisvert (@bunny_poems.jpeg).

"A Dreamless Sleep" was previously published by *Discretionary Love,* September 2023.

"The Lunar Light Within" was previously published in *TulipTree Review's* Spring/Summer 2023 Wild Women Issue (#13).

"The stars talk about us, too" is based on a prompt from Hazel Knight (@hazel.poetry).

"Multiple Choice for the Grieving Heart" is written after "Multiple Choice for Adrift Michigander" by Brian Czyzyk, published in *Poetry*, February 2022; and is based on a prompt from Amy Kay (@amykaypoetry).

"Where did I get my heart from?" is written after "Still Here" by Kyron Rashād (@kyronrashad.wav) from the album "a foolish story about an imposter," 2023.

"This Season of Life" is based on a prompt from Michelle Awad (@theconstantpoet).

"The Essentials" was written after "15 Things A Man Should Own" by Tom Ford and Holly Macnaghten, published in *Gentlemen's Journal*; and after "The Essentials" by Seneca Basoalto (@senecabasoalto).

ACKNOWLEDGEMENTS

To Frances Story (Poet Jen Harris), my dear friend, my creative sibling, my book doula: I will never forget the first time I read a poem aloud to an audience that included you. In a quiet pause between stanzas, your voice in the back called out, "Speak, Poet." Your affirmation was my baptism. I didn't believe I could be a poet until you reminded me I already was. Thank you, from the bottom of my heart. None of this would have been possible without your time, wisdom, and unwavering belief in me. I am so grateful for your love and friendship.

To my beta readers Kate Mapother, Amanda Roth, Jenn Stark, Irina Bogomolova, Kathryn Moon, Kennedi Jones, and April Renee: Thank you for reading the raw version of this manuscript with such care, and for sharing your helpful feedback. These poems are stronger because of your insight. Thank you.

To Samantha Peters: Thank you for turning this Google doc into an actual book and ebook! This book is real because of you. I'm so grateful for your help in creating this book.

To Bobbi Stark: Thank you for creating such an incredible piece of artwork for the cover of my debut collection of poetry. You're a phenomenal artist and an amazing friend, and I'm grateful to know you.

To the many wonderful members of The Writing Workshop KC: Thank you for being my creative home. Your encouragement and camaraderie mean the world to me. Many of the poems in this book began as shitty first drafts that I wrote and shared in class. Thank you for holding them so tenderly and believing in them – and in me. See y'all next Tuesday!

To my mother, Joyce Trumbull; my father, Phil Trumbull; and my brother, Ian Trumbull: Thank you for your unconditional love. Thank you for supporting me in everything I do. Thank you for always believing in me, from the very beginning. Thank you for being the lighthouse that shows me the way back home – to you, and to myself.

To Miles, my best friend and life partner: Thank you for building this life with me. Thank you for believing in me and my poems. Thank you for taking on extra tasks so that I could work on this book. Thank you for attending open mics and award ceremonies. Thank you for loving me in the radical, incredible ways you do. Thank you for everything.

To Megan, my girlfriend and partner: Thank you for being my friend, my lover, and my muse. Thank you for trying something new with me. Thank you for your constant love, support, encouragement, and patience as I wrote this book. Thank you for being you.

To Kyron Rashād, my creative sibling: Thank you for believing in me and this book. Creative kinship is so rare and so beautiful – thank you for sharing it with me. It is such a blessing to be writing and growing alongside you.

To my wonderful friends Natalie Smyth, Amanda Bignall, Laura Fariole, Mayra Aviña, Ryrick Lippke, Lizz Mueller, Alyssa Bennett Smith, Allison Sage, May Robertson, Loraine Ruetz, Isabel Walsh, Stephanie Pyle, Paul DeCorte, and Adam Wisniewski: Thank you for bringing such joy and beauty into my life. Thank you for all the love and support you all have given me over the years. Thank you for being my cheerleaders. Thank you for giving me a safe place to land. And thank you for inspiring the poem "Platonic Love."

To all the versions of me who fought hard to get here, dreamed these poems into life, and put in the work to birth this beautiful book: Thank you. Thank you. Thank you.

ABOUT THE AUTHOR

Jess Whetsel is a poet, writer, editor, and public speaker based in Toledo, Ohio on Erie, Kickapoo, Seneca, and Odawa land. She earned her bachelor's degree in English Creative Writing and German from Denison University, and her Master of Social Work degree from the University of Denver. Her poetry has appeared in the literary journals *Tulip Tree Review* and *Discretionary Love. A Softer Kind of Audacity* is her debut poetry collection. You can learn more about Whetsel and her work on her website, www.jesswhetsel.com, or by following her Instagram, @jesswhetselwrites.

Printed in the USA
CPSIA information can be obtained
at www.ICGtesting.com
CBHW010818141123
1855CB00022B/103